Francis *of* Assisi
Living Fortitude

SAINTS & VIRTUES

Francis *of* Assisi
Living Fortitude

ave maria press AMP Notre Dame, Indiana

© 2005 by Ave Maria Press, Inc.

www.avemariapress.com

International Standard Book Number: 1-59471-060-0

Author of biography of St. Francis of Assisi: Boniface Hanley, O.F.M.

Project Editor: Michael Amodei

Cover and text design by Brian C. Conley

Printed and bound in the United States of America.

Photo Credits
© Greg Friedman, o.f.m. – 19, 22, 27, 31, 32, 34
© The Crosiers/ Gene Plaisted, o.s.c. – 6, 8, 38

Contents

Virtue

A virtue is a good habit that helps us to live the Christian life.

Fortitude

Fortitude is the virtue that enables us to conquer our fears, even the fear of death, and to face trials and persecutions.

St. Francis of Assisi

Francis Bernardone was born in the town of Assisi, located in Umbria, Italy, sometime during 1181 or 1182.

Francis's baptismal name was John.

Francis's father, Peter, was a wealthy clothing merchant. His mother, Pica, was from an upper class family.

Around the age of twenty, Francis was taken prisoner in a war between the cities of Perugia and Assisi. The experience deepened his dream to become a knight.

While on his way to battle, he met a poor, sick man. Francis was touched by the experience and it changed his life.

From that time on, Francis was devoted to love for Jesus Christ through service to what he called "Lady Poverty."

Francis attracted eleven other men from Assisi to follow him, founding the Franciscan community, which by the time of his death had thousands of male and female members.

Francis died on October 3, 1226.

Francis was canonized a saint in 1228.

He is one of the most popular and beloved saints.

INTRODUCTION:
BROTHER
Francis

Listen, little poor ones, whom the
    Lord has called,
who have come together from all parts of
    the world;

May the truth unite you, so that when
    you die,
on complete obedience your trust may
    rely.

Look not to the outside for the life you
    live;
better far the bounty that the Spirit
    will give.

In great love, I beg you; use God's gifts
    with grace,
so that those who suffer ills may bear
    them in peace.

You will sell your burdens at a higher
    price,
and as queens in heaven you will wear
    crowns of life.

—ST. FRANCIS OF ASSISI,
WRITTEN TO ST. CLARE PRIOR TO HIS DEATH

t. Francis of Assisi was a dreamer. From a young age, he desired glory. Led by this dream he became a soldier. He fought in one battle, though his side was defeated and he was captured and taken as a prisoner of war. He was kept in a dungeon for many months and became very sick. But Francis's dreams never left him in prison; they only changed some. Glory began to take on a new meaning.

Francis's new dreams involved serving God, not his military superiors. His new dreams involved loving the poor, not worldly riches. His new dreams led him into conflict with his family. His new dreams led Francis to seek out suffering and persecution, not to avoid them.

Suffering everything in the defense of your faith is part of living the human virtue called *fortitude*.

Fortitude is the virtue that helps us to face difficulties and remain constant in our pursuit of goodness. Many of the difficulties we face come as temptations to do evil and avoid good. The teenage and young adult years are filled with temptations in many areas—for example, to have sex, to cheat, or to abuse drugs and alcohol. The gift of fortitude helps us to persevere for the good.

There is an added dimension to the virtue of fortitude that goes beyond helping us to avoid our daily temptations. Fortitude helps us to conquer the fear of death, and to face severe trials and persecutions that come with being a faithful Christian. Fortitude can even help us to give up our entire life for the cause of truth and goodness.

In order to pursue his new dreams, Francis relied on the gift of fortitude. Francis's father, Peter, had planned for Francis to take over his clothing business. Francis had no such plans.

Eventually Francis's love for the poor led to a split between father and son, a cause of deep bitterness and suffering. But Francis persevered, stripping himself of his material possessions for his newfound love of the poor.

Near the end of his life, in August, 1224, Francis prayed to share the sufferings Christ bore on the cross. In a little cell he had carved out at Mount Alvernia, Francis received the same five wounds of Christ on his hands, feet, and side. This *stigmata* was a cause of physical pain and weakness in the last two years of his life. Yet Francis carried on in faith, aided by the gift of fortitude so that he was able to write the words of the song to St. Clare before he died: "Look not to the outside for the life you live; better far the bounty that the Spirit will give."

The following pages are a brief biographical sketch of St. Francis of Assisi. *Read about his life.* Try to take just one or two sittings over the course of one day to read pages 15–41.

Next, *pray with St. Francis.* Pages 43–50 offer a five day prayer meditation based on his life and writing.

Finally, *live the virtue of fortitude* as exemplified by St. Francis. Pages 53–61 provide some ideas. Keep a short journal to mark how well you do.

the LIFE of FRANCIS

"*I*'m in the clothing business," Peter Bernardone would have said, had you asked. And he would have liked that you asked!

Mr. Bernardone would have also liked you to ask about his family, for he had an Italian's deep pride in his three children. He especially prized one son and completely spoiled him. This was Francis, now in his early twenties and already doing well in the family enterprises.

Peter Bernardone got a real kick out of his son. The youth knew how to live, what he wanted, and how to get it. Nature had endowed him with fairly good looks, a personality that attracted and held friends, and a flair for good-humored leadership. None of these qualities would hurt his business career.

Unfortunately for Peter, it was this son, his favorite, who would break his heart. The boy turned on his father and in a nasty family rift that eventually boiled into a public scene, Francis walked out of his father's business and his father's life. Francis left the fire of his father's pride to die down to cold, bitter ashes.

Things like this happen in families, but never for quite the same reasons, nor with the same consequences as in the family of Peter Bernardone, resident and wealthy merchant of Assisi, Italy, in the early thirteenth century.

Facing Life's Big Questions

One might trace the roots of the Bernardone family discord and the consequent amazing events of Francis's life to his entry into military service in 1202 when he was twenty years old. Previous to this time, Francis gave little indication that he was to swerve so radically from the course that his parents had so fondly set for him.

After his enlistment he fought bravely in one bloody battle, but his troops suffered defeat. Taken as a prisoner of war, he was held captive for several months, then released and sent home. His father and mother cried with joy, and made up for the long months of suffering by showering him with affection and (what was even more important to Francis at the time) by spending lots of money.

But the months spent in the prison dungeon had affected Francis's health. He became so sick that he almost died and he had to convalesce for an entire year. It was during this time that, perhaps for the first time ever, he did some serious thinking about the meaning of life. He probed the age-old dilemmas: Who am I? Where do I come from? Where am I going? What is this world? What is love?

Francis was an Italian, a Catholic, and a born poet. As an Italian, his soul was moved naturally to deep affection, love, and joy. His faith supplied him with crystal-clear answers to his questions. And as a poet, he could see right through to the fearsome ramifications of those answers. What he saw frightened him and—as many have done before and since—he shied away from deeper thinking for a time.

When his health was restored, Francis reentered the social scene of the young and rich of Assisi. That meant one thing: parties, and lots of them. Always at the center of all the fun, Francis drove himself into the very vortex of the revelry, leaving behind his deeper concerns in the hope that merrymaking would make him happy.

Listening to Dreams

One night as Francis slept he saw in a dream the house where he was born changed into a stately palace. The walls of the palace were hung with magnificent armor, banners, shields, and swords—all the trophies of medieval warfare. A voice, remarkably clear and coherent, explained that this was to be his palace, the gathering place for his knights. The arms were theirs, the banners the tokens of their innumerable conquests. To complete this wonderful vision, a beautiful bride awaited Francis.

Francis woke in a happy sweat. He knew then he was destined for glory—the kind he thought he really wanted.

A few mornings later Francis left Assisi to go to southern Italy to enlist again as a soldier. He got as far as Spoleto, a day's journey, bivouacked, slept, and dreamt once more. Again he heard the same voice as before, but this time it asked questions.

"Francis, who can do more for you, the servant or the master?"

Francis, enjoying some sense of practical politics, answered, "Why, the master!"

And then came the dialogue that changed the course of Francis's life, and in many ways the course of human history. "Why, then," the voice exclaimed, "are you seeking the servant instead of the master, the vassal instead of the prince?"

Francis, recognizing the voice as that of Christ, suddenly grew weary of retreating from him.

"Lord," he asked tiredly, "what will you have me do?"

"Return home," the answer came. "Your vision will have its spiritual fulfillment through me."

And so the would-be warrior returned to Assisi. Although his friends and peers were happy that he had returned, they soon sensed that the wild Francis had changed. Something was quite evidently troubling him. Shadows passed quickly across his bright face, and sometimes his smile would harden while his crackling eyes would go dull. His friends concluded that the inevitable had happened: Francis had fallen in love. His friends couldn't refrain from asking him about it.

"Who is she, Francis? Oh, who is she?" they demanded to know.

Francis had to answer, but how could he tell them that he was in love with one whom he hardly knew and of whom he was more than a little afraid? So he said to his friends: "I do dream of taking a wife and she whom I shall marry is so noble, so rich, so fair, and so wise, that not one of you has seen her like."

This love of Francis's life was Lady Poverty.

Embracing His Call

Francis had developed a habit of slipping away from the city and entering one of the many caves near Assisi. Sometimes a friend who understood Francis's new vocation would accompany him on retreat, but Francis always entered the cave and stayed alone.

One day Francis went inside a cave and his final surrender was made. He accepted Lady Poverty as his bride, on the terms that God demanded: the living of the holy gospel.

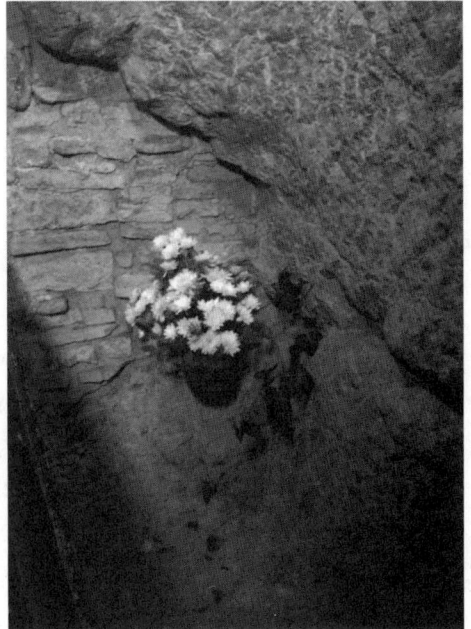

CAVE OF ST. FRANCIS AT CARCERI

Francis emerged from the cave with his face flushed and beaming as one in love. In his simplicity and youth he perhaps hardly understood what he had promised. But sincerely he vowed to fulfill whatever his spouse would demand of him.

Francis then made a pilgrimage to Rome, emptied his purse in almsgiving, and gave his expensive clothes to an eager beggar. Then, dressed in rags, he joined a group of bums. He was happy. He was one with the poor.

After a short time in Rome, he returned to Assisi to face a curious temptation. To understand his trial, it is important to remember that the son of Peter Bernardone had been raised a privileged child of his times. He was brought up in a certain social set, proud of his manners, and neat and fastidious in his clothing and care of his body. Like most young men, he was concerned about how he looked and his physical prowess more than he might have dared to admit.

One by one the values of his upbringing were attacked by the poverty that he had pledged. Francis yielded as gracefully as he could to giving away his clothing, joining with beggars, and swallowing his fierce Italian pride. None of this came easy. And yet one thing—his body—was left to renounce, and Francis found this the most difficult. "It seemed to me a bitter thing," he said. And then Francis faced a situation that brought his fear to a forefront.

Europe in those days was full of people suffering from leprosy, a very contagious disease that literally eats away at the skin, leaving open sores. Feared and despised, lepers crept from one edge of the town to another, seeking food and shelter. They wore a bell tied around their necks to warn people that they were approaching.

One day at a crossroads near Assisi, Francis suddenly came face to face with one of these tragic invalids. The young Francis recoiled in fear and panic and almost immediately the situation became clear to him. It was, he knew, now or never that he must give up his love for his body and physical beauty.

Francis returned to the leper, embraced the astonished outcast, and pressed some money into his diseased hands. Francis had now set his course and, typically, he rushed to its logical conclusion. He left the leper and went searching for more, finding a hospital full of lepers. He gathered these amazed pariahs of society together and begged their pardon for having held them in disgust. He promised to come to them and serve their needs.

Then, giving them what money he had, he kissed each one on the mouth and left.

Repairing God's Church

If it was money that Francis hated, it was money that did him a final service. Money broke Francis's connection with his home.

One day Francis was passing the tiny, half-ruined chapel of St. Damian just outside of Assisi. He entered the place and knelt before a simple Byzantine crucifix to pray. Suddenly Christ spoke to him from the cross saying "Francis, go and repair my Church, which, as you see, is falling into ruin."

In his utter simplicity Francis accepted the command for what it was. The chapel was in poor condition; it was God's house. Therefore, he reasoned, this is the place I must repair.

His first need was money and, as usual, Francis went to his father. But Peter Bernardone had left home on a business trip. With some disregard for the seventh commandment, Francis went down to his father's shop, loaded his horse with cloth, and left on his own business trip. He sold the materials and returned to the

SAN DAMIANO AT ASSISI WAS THE FIRST CHURCH THAT FRANCIS RESTORED.

chapel of St. Damian. The poor, aged priest who tended the chapel was overwhelmed by Francis. First, Francis kissed his hands and pressed a sack of gold into them. Then he announced that he was going to repair the priest's church! Poverty had not dulled the prudence of this priest. He absolutely refused the money and looked with suspicious eyes on Francis, whose reputation prior to this had hardly been that of one who worked around churches.

Francis exercised a bit of prudence of his own. He located a hiding place in the nearby hills where he would remain, rather than going home to face the wrath of his father, which was sure to come.

Francis and his Father

When Peter Bernardone returned and discovered the theft and flight of his son, he flew from the shop in a blind rage and charged toward St. Damian's. Neighbors who had spent days in delicious anticipation of an ugly scene between father and son poured into the streets, taking sides, laughing, and sneering— all thoroughly enjoying themselves—as they too made their way to St. Damian's.

So noisily did this troop bear down on the chapel that Francis heard them coming in plenty of time to scurry to his hiding place. The priest did not know the location of Francis's hideout so when Peter asked where his son was the priest could truthfully say that he did not know. Peter Bernardone—whose anger was now compounded by frustration—stomped back to Assisi with his disappointed audience.

Francis held out for some days and then straggled into town to face the showdown. The people of Assisi must have been shocked when they saw him. Thin and pale, his clothes rough and his hands hard from labor, he looked like a madman. Street toughs began pelting him with rocks and mud and the inevitable crowd gathered (in it were many of his friends). Many people began to jeer and shout at him. Francis's father heard the uproar, saw who was at the center of it, and, completely distraught by the indignities heaped by his son on the good name of the family, tore into the middle of the pack. With shouts, blows, and kicks, he drove Francis into the house. To prevent any further nonsense, Peter chained his son in the cellar.

Some days later Peter left on another business trip. Francis's long-suffering mother, who continued to love her son despite the embarrassments he had caused, unchained Francis and let him escape his prison. Like a homing pigeon he flew—right back to St. Damian's.

With this latest insult to his parental authority, Peter Bernardone's patience gave way. He appealed for civil prosecution of his son for the theft of his property. Francis rejected the summons of the magistrate on the grounds that as a servant of God he was only under the jurisdiction of the Bishop of Assisi, Lord Guido. Francis's appeal was upheld and the case was transferred to Church jurisdiction. The bishop ordered a public trial to be conducted on the plaza in front of the bishop's palace. The family's dirty linen was to be washed in public and the people of Assisi loved it.

At the palace, moments before the trial was to take place, Lord Guido explained to Francis his position before the law. "Stealing," the bishop counseled, "regardless of its purpose, is wrong." He suggested that Francis return what money he had that belonged to his father.

Francis agreed and added, "I will do even more."

Stripping himself down to a haircloth wrapped around his waist, the intractable young man picked up the heap of clothing and walked onto the plaza to face his father and the curious crowd. If it was a scene his father wanted, Francis would provide him with one. However, Francis was not doing any of this for show. He was dreadfully and devastatingly sincere.

He called out: "Listen well, all of you—until now I called Peter Bernardone 'father.' But now that I wish to serve God I return to him not only his money that he so much desires, but the clothes, too, that I had from him."

Francis threw the clothing and the money in a heap on the plaza. "Now I will truly be able to say 'Our Father who art in heaven' and not 'My father Peter Bernardone.'"

Next something even more shameful happened. Peter Bernardone bent down and scooped up the money and the clothing and left, hurling curses and other hateful comments over his shoulder. The trial was over.

There and Back Again

Clad only in a threadbare gardener's cloak which the bishop had given him to cover himself, Francis left Assisi. He headed into the mountains surrounding the town—exactly why, it is difficult to say. Many times in his life he experienced an almost overwhelming hunger for solitude. No doubt after the bitter events on Assisi's plaza he needed some time to sort things out.

Francis's time spent in the mountains was far from tranquil, however. A band of thieves ambushed him and, finding he had nothing, threw him into a ravine full of snow. Wet and cold, Francis climbed up out of the snowy cleft and made his way to a monastery where the monks gave him shelter and precious little else in exchange for his labors as a kitchen boy. Sheer cold and hunger drove Francis from this inhospitable monastery. He journeyed to Gubbio, a village near Assisi, where an old friend of his gave Francis a cast-off hermit's habit. Thus clad, Francis returned to St. Damian's and continued the restoration of the damaged church.

Possessing no money, Francis begged in Assisi for supplies like rocks, mortar, wood, and other basic materials, along with the food he needed. Gradually the barrage of jibes and curses and pelting died out as the townspeople got used to Francis and his begging.

We should remember not to judge the people of Assisi too harshly. After all, Francis had not only defied his parents and stolen their property, but he was also continuing his contact with the contagious lepers. That these people dealt with him at all is a tribute to them. But eventually, as natural Italian courtesy asserted itself, the people of Assisi began to grow fond of the bedraggled Francis.

Francis was the main reason for the change in their attitude. With piercing knowledge of his own sins, he refused to consider the insults and rocks hurled at him as anything other than what he deserved. Those who perpetrated these actions he saw as friends who had the courage to tell him the truth. If he had retaliated in any way or acted grim against their behaviors, he would have only enraged them further. As a result of the honest conviction of his own sinfulness, he bore his ostracism joyfully and courteously. And while he had chosen a bitter road for himself, he neither despised people for not following him, nor did he urge anyone to join him. In short, he minded his own mysterious business.

Amazed by humility, the people of Assisi found it a pleasant thing to see Francis. A meeting with him somehow made one's whole day brighter. If a person offered him a bit of bread, a piece of wood, or even a stone, Francis would give back a sweet blessing from deep in his heart. "Give me a stone," he would cry, "and God will bless you. Give me two stones and God will twice bless you."

For Francis, the relief of living honestly the life God had called him to—the life of poverty—was so great that he could not help but enjoy himself. In a ferment of love for Lady Poverty, he would often bubble out into song. From sheer exuberance he formed a mock violin from two pieces of wood and sang the praises of his wonderful God and God's daughter, Lady Poverty.

For the next two or three years, Francis restored chapels (he did at least three), begged for food and materials, and served the lepers.

And then, God complicated his life.

The Franciscan Movement Begins

Francis was at Mass at one of the chapels he had restored— St. Mary of the Angels—on the feast of St. Matthias in 1209. God revealed to him through the gospel reading of the day (Matthew 10:7-19) what was to be his full life's work. Jesus' words were to become the blueprint by which Francis would live his life:

Cure the sick, raise the dead, cleanse lepers, drive out demons. Without cost you have received; without cost you are to give. Do not take gold or silver or copper for your belts, no sack for the journey, a second tunic, or a walking stick. The laborer deserves his keep.

After Mass, Francis asked the priest to explain this gospel to him. The priest told him it meant that the disciples of Christ must possess nothing—neither money, food, nor excess clothing. They were simply to preach the good news of kingdom of God and do penance for sin. The words of this gospel reading were the catalyst that brought the Franciscan movement into being.

Francis trembled with enthusiasm and exclaimed: "This is what I long with all my inmost heart to do." In his typical directness, he cast off what he considered to be excess clothing—his shoes, belt, and mantle. He wore instead a simple tunic

FRANCIS'S HABIT IN THE RELIC CASE, AT THE BASILICA OF ST. CLARE

bound about his middle with a cord. Later—as he never was in excellent health—the chill of the Italian winter forced him to wear a cloak, but it was one that he had made himself.

Francis began to preach before the people of Assisi—an act of supreme humility. Knowing that the townspeople were busy, he made his sermons brief and simple. His natural charm and warm, sympathetic personality became a vehicle of God's grace. Francis's goodness lay naked before Assisi, and to its everlasting credit, Assisi accepted him for what he was.

Within the next year, eleven men slipped silently from various strata of society and asked Francis if they could be his companions and to live as he lived. Some brought talents, others money, and a few nothing but their sins. Francis took them all on the condition that they give away *everything*: their money to the poor, their wills to a superior (they took turns as superior), and their addiction to sin to God.

These first followers came as a result of witnessing Francis's own marriage to Lady Poverty. There would be more and more that would follow during his own life and to this day. One night in a dream, Francis saw them all:

A great multitude of men . . . their footfalls still resound in my ears as they come and go according to the commands of holy obedience. The highroads are crowded with them, coming to this place (Assisi), from almost every nation. There are Frenchmen coming, Spaniards hurrying, Germans and Englishmen running, and a tremendous throng speaking various other tongues hasten there.

Francis's Rule of Life

In 1209 Francis wrote a Rule of Life for his present and future brothers. Composed of gospel texts and a few precepts, this Rule aimed to guide these men to walk literally in the footsteps of Christ.

This concept of the literal imitation of Christ demanded a departure from forms of religious life known in the Catholic Church up to that time. For many centuries the monastic system had effectively served the Church. Monasteries were well-established institutions within which monks sought religious perfection by living a well-ordered routine of work and prayer. While each monk took his vows of obedience, chastity, and poverty, the monastery as a legal entity was able to own property and other things. The monks supported themselves by their own work. Always advancing as disciplined, orderly, and organized colonies of Christ, the monks preserved and propagated the Catholic religion in the midst of barbarian invasions and feudal wars.

How Francis differed from the monastery approach was that he saw the world as his follower's monastery. Rather than bind them to the exquisitely organized cloisters of monastic discipline, he was inspired by God and the needs of his time to send his men into the frightfully disorganized world. If the world was to be their cloister than their bodies were to be their cells. Food and clothing were not to be a concern, for the heavenly Father who sent them was to provide for their needs. They were to live the gospel and by their own poverty and humility give a Christ-like example to men suffering under the burden of sin. Their work was to be whatever the needs of the Church demanded.

Francis called his followers the Little Brothers, *Frati Minori,* a name which remains with the Franciscans today in the title Friars Minor. Francis insisted on seeking approval of this form of life from Pope Innocent III. In 1202 he set out with his group of followers—now twelve—for Rome.

Pope Innocent was at first reluctant to approve to this novel form of religious life. The prudent thing for him to do was to ignore Francis and the request. And that is what he did—at first. But even popes sleep and dream, and during the night after his interview with Francis, Pope Innocent had a strange dream. He saw the huge Roman basilica of St. John Lateran, the Mother Church of Christendom, quaking on its ancient foundations and threatening to lean over and fall like a great tree before a storm. Suddenly a little man appeared and threw his thin body against the toppling structure and alone held it up before the nameless furies threatening it. The face of the little man was plain: it was that of Francis, the man who had petitioned the pope just the day before.

It is not usually prudent for a pope to change a decision based on a dream, but Innocent sent for Francis, and listened to him more carefully. Like most others, Innocent was touched by Francis's personality. Nevertheless, he still consulted his advisers. They concluded with the pope that Francis's revolutionary ideas had merit and that to deny their validity would be to deny that one could live a life described as ideal in the gospels. Innocent gave his verbal endorsement and promised more definite approval if Francis's plan proved practical.

Ten years later Francis's order numbered more than three thousand men.

Clare Joins Francis

Returning to Assisi with papal approval for their way of life, the friars took up quarters in an abandoned mule shed until a thoughtless peasant, wishing to shelter his mule, drove the friars out. Francis led them back to St. Mary of the Angels

Chapel, which was given to the friars by the Benedictine monks. This chapel became their headquarters. They lived in mud huts around it and continued their prayers, penance, preaching, and labors. Other men continued to come and join them.

Francis had little problem incorporating men who wished to follow his life into the community, but soon women wanted to follow too. What would Francis do with women? The person who tested Francis was a woman whose blood was noble and whose will was steel. Her name was Clare di Favorone and she was eighteen years old.

VESTMENT THOUGHT TO BE MADE BY ST. CLARE FOR ST. FRANCIS.

Clare had probably heard Francis speak on various occasions in Assisi, and one day she confided her difficulties to him. She explained her reasons for not marrying. Not only did she desire to give her life and love completely to God, she also had determined to live in the same poverty as Francis and the brothers. Within a short time Clare made her decision to break with her family and the world and to follow the road that Francis mapped out for her.

On Palm Sunday in 1212, while her family was dining, Clare slipped out a back door traditionally reserved only for carrying out the family dead, and in the darkness of the night met another woman and accomplice, the Lady Pacifica. The two women then made their way to St. Mary of the Angels Chapel where Francis and some of the other friars awaited them. By candlelight, Francis snipped off Clare's long golden locks of hair. Pacifica slipped a rough brown robe over Clare's feast day dress, fastened it around her waist with a rope, and then covered her shorn head with a black veil. Clare pronounced her vows of poverty, chastity, and obedience to God. In this romantic and improbable fashion the Second Order of St. Francis—known as the Poor Clares or the Poor Ladies of Assisi—was founded. Also during this time, it is likely that Francis founded a Third Order of Franciscans for lay men and women living in the world.

BASILICA OF ST. CLARE

Francis Reforms the Church

Francis's interpreted his original call as an invitation to rebuild the physical church at St. Damian's. Though he would have never acknowledged it during his lifetime, Francis's larger work was to reform the Church throughout the world.

As the years passed, the fame of Francis and his friars spread throughout Italy. The leaven was at work in the masses. His arrival in the little towns was always an occasion of great celebration. Bells would ring and people would flock to the plaza to hear him preach. Francis was not a reformer who moved in a cloud of gloom. He bubbled with life and the Italians rejoiced with him. He never argued with heretics, flailed at sinners, or preached God's wrath. Rather, Francis spoke courteously to all about Jesus Christ and about the virtues and vices he saw in each of them. All creation was to Francis proof of God's goodness. The universe was Christ's kingdom.

Francis knew few fears in his life, but there was one that constantly plagued him: the fear of becoming a hypocrite. He knew that the best sermons his friars could preach were the examples of their own lives and he was painfully aware that the validity of his mission to restore the gospel as a way of life for all would rest on his ability to live it himself. Once when he was ill (as he often was) Francis's superior ordered him to sew a piece of fox fur inside his habit to protect him against the cold. He obeyed but pleaded and was granted permission to sew another piece on the outside of the habit so that people could see how Francis of Assisi pampered himself. In this, and a myriad of other actions, Francis lived the motto "Preach the gospel always. When necessary, use words."

How the Franciscans Were "Organized"

To understand Francis's success as a religious reformer, one must grasp the utter simplicity of his movement. Religious reform, he insisted, must begin with one's self, and he demanded this of everyone who joined his order. While aware of human weakness, Francis allowed no deviation from the ideal on the part of the friars. His way of life, he felt, was simple enough—to live the gospel. He had little patience with any other schemes, plans, or levels of organization.

It is also significant that while Francis passionately loved all of nature, he could never quite warm up to ants. Ants were simply too tightly organized and frantically industrious to suit him. His religious order as he conceived it could hardly be described as an "organization." Rather, it simply existed to give the world an example of Christ-like living. The specifics he preferred to leave to the circumstances of time and place and the ingenuity of his friars. Love and the gospel, he knew, must always find a way to manifest themselves.

STATUE OF FRANCIS IN THE COURTYARD OF THE BISHOP OF ASSISI

St. Dominic, who had brilliantly organized a new Order of Preachers (Dominicans) at about the same time the Franciscans were founded, attempted to persuade Francis to unite both communities to form one great order. What the Franciscans patently lacked—namely, refined and efficient organization—Dominic Guzman knew he could provide. Dominic must have thrilled at the possibilities of such a union, but Francis was too simple and too certain of the role Christ wished his order to assume in the Church. He rejected the great Dominic's proposal. But this act destroyed neither Dominic's respect nor affection for Francis. The two founders, according to tradition, were friends.

By 1217, however, the Franciscan order had grown to such proportions that Francis had to impose some vague outlines of organization. He established territorial divisions (provinces) and superiors. But the saint insisted that the chain of command he forged be not of the steel of obedience, but of the fire of love. Hence he called his superiors neither prior, abbot, or superior, but *ministers* and defined their duties as "servants of the rest of the brethren."

Twice a year—at Pentecost and the feast of St. Michael (near the end of September)—Francis called the friars back to Assisi for a general gathering or chapter. At these reunions the policies of the order, its development, and its various problems were discussed.

It was at the 1217 Pentecost Chapter that Francis decided to send brethren outside of Italy to both pagan and Christian lands. The missionary effort lacked organization. It began with men who simply volunteered and went to far off places by foot. Superiors were chosen and the friars moved out to France, Spain, Germany, Hungary, Portugal, Syria, and the Near East. One hundred years after the 1217 Pentecost Chapter, more than thirty thousand friars were living in all parts of Europe. Also, Franciscans had penetrated and successfully established missions in the uncharted and pagan kingdoms of the Near, Middle, and Far East.

In 1219, Francis himself left Italy on one of the most incredible missionary ventures in the annals of the Church. He journeyed to Damietta, Egypt, where the Christian crusaders were locked in vicious warfare with the nomadic Moslem people, the Saracens. There he crossed the battle lines, somehow survived inside the Saracen camp, and procured an interview with Melek-el-kamel, the Sultan and commander-in-chief of the Muslim forces. He proposed that the Sultan be baptized a Christian. Surprisingly enough, the Sultan gave serious consideration to Francis's plea. Finally, he reluctantly rejected the proposal, knowing that the Saracens would take a dim view of such a defection. Nevertheless he did grant Francis and his followers permission to journey and preach throughout Egypt. It was at this time that Francis visited the Holy Land and prayed at those places made sacred by the presence of Christ.

The Order Continues to Grow

Meanwhile the order continued its uninhibited growth. But with the rapid expansion came a series of complications and difficulties that threatened to destroy the work Francis had so effectively begun.

The pioneer days of the order, when a small number of friars drew their inspiration from regular contact with Francis, had ended. Now, with the order numbering thousands and already sinking its roots in foreign soil, many a friar had never even met Francis, much less had the opportunity to draw inspiration from contact with him. It became increasingly evident that more detailed legislation must be provided if the Order of the Little Brothers was to fulfill its mission in the Church. Summoned back to Assisi from the Holy Land to face the problems of growth, Francis called a General Chapter in 1220 in which he resigned as Minister General so that he could devote himself entirely to preparing a more detailed rule of life for his friars.

The next three years, during which Francis labored to develop the Franciscan Rule, were a period of great stress in his life. Although not well equipped by temperament or training to be a lawmaker, he had set himself a formidable legislative goal. He determined to produce a rule that would permit his friars to live the holy gospel with the greatest amount of individual liberty and minimal regulation.

Francis's burden was not lightened by certain friars who were very vocal with their own ideas about the future development of the order and Francis's ability to guide it. Fortunately, the Holy See helped to rescue Francis and the friars from their confusion. Pope Gregory IX became, at Francis's request, protector of the order and guided Francis to completion of the Rule of 1223, which the order observes to this day.

Dying Like Christ

The struggle to prevent the dissolution of his order, to salvage his ideals, and to keep them at the core and center of his new Franciscan Rule of Life (which he did) all exacted its inexorable toll on the already fragile health of Francis. He began to realize that he was nearing the end of his time on earth.

As death (or as Francis preferred, "Sister Death") hovered ever closer to him, he became obsessed with one idea. He had lived more like Christ than any man before or since; now he begged to die like Christ. And he knew that this would demand a miracle.

In August 1224, Francis retired with some friars to a mountain called Alvernia in Umbria, near Assisi. The Italian summer days softened one into another as the saint entered into a mystical union with Christ that can't be adequately described. So intense were the exchanges of love that Francis began to share with Christ the sufferings of Calvary. Frightful as the request was, Christ granted it to Francis, and in an awesome vision, the Crucified Christ embraced him and poured into Francis's soul—and his fragile body—the black horrors of the first Good Friday. When Francis stepped back from this embrace he saw his miracle. Christ had cut into his body the same five wounds that he had suffered on the cross. They were the stigmata, the red seals of divine approval pressed into the hands and feet and side of Francis of Assisi.

FRANCIS RECEIVES THE STIGMATA—THE IMPRESSION OF THE FIVE WOUNDS OF CHRIST—ON HIS BODY.

Francis Sings

During the last two years of his life Francis's cup of physical suffering was filled up, pressed down, and ran over. His health broke. Spleen, liver, stomach, and eyes throbbed in the

discordant rhythm of pain. His whole system was lashed by recurrent bouts of malaria he had contracted in Egypt. Efforts of physicians to comfort and cure him, if sincere, were most crude. The doctors, for instance, applied red-hot irons to his temples to relieve the pain in his eyes—an ordeal he endured with grace because "Brother Fire" had acknowledged Francis's plea not to hurt him.

But it was during these last days when his body was racked with the most pain, that Francis began to understand his bodily antagonist for what it really was—the gift of God to man. As his spirit rose above the crags and peaks of pain, he pulled what rags of bodily strength were left in him and broke into his own song to nature, the magnificent Canticle of the Sun:

Most high, almighty, good Lord!
All praise, glory, honor and exaltation are yours!
To you alone do they belong,
and no mere mortal dares pronounce your Name.
Praise to you, O Lord our God, for all your creatures
first, for our dear Brother Sun,
who gives us the day
and illumines us with his light;
fair is he, in splendor radiant,
bearing your very likeness, O Lord.
For our Sister Moon,
and for the bright, shining stars:
We praise you, O Lord.
For our Brother Wind,
and fair and stormy seasons
and all heaven's varied moods,
by which you nourish all that you have made:

We praise you, O Lord.
For our Brother Fire,
who brightens up our darkest nights;
beautiful is he and eager,
invincible and keen:
We praise you, O Lord.
For our Mother Earth,
who sustains and feeds us,
producing fair fruits, many-colored flowers and herbs:
We praise you, O Lord.
For those who forgive one another for love of you,
and who patiently bear sickness and other trials.
Happy are they who peacefully endure;
you will crown them, O Most High!
We praise you, O Lord.
For our Sister Death,
the inescapable fact of life.
Woe to those who die in mortal sin!
Happy are those she finds doing your will!
From the Second Death they stand immune:
We praise you, O Lord.
All creatures,
praise and glorify my Lord.
Give him thanks
and serve him in great humility.
We praise you, O Lord.

There was not merely *something* of the poet, knight, and saint in Francis, there was *everything* of these in him. Poet, knight, and saint he was to the last—this simple, courageous man.

It was during his illness that Francis felt a greater need to sing than ever before. Nothing assuaged his pain like the sound of a stanza of verse. Therefore he continually asked his attendant friars to intone lauds and psalms.

Friar Elias chided Francis gently because he was concerned about public opinion: "How can you show so much gaiety when you should be thinking of death?" he asked Francis. Francis replied:

> *I have been thinking of my end night and day for so long! From the time you had that vision in Foligno and you told me that I had only two more years to live, from that time I have never ceased to think about death. Let me now rejoice in the Lord and in the praises sung to him for my infirmities.*

Francis's end came on October 3, 1226, near sundown. He died singing.

pray with FRANCIS

The Morning and Evening Prayers are adapted from St. Francis of Assisi's paraphrase of the Our Father. The Thoughts for the Day are taken from the letters, poems, and songs of St. Francis.

* Allow ten minutes for quiet prayer at the beginning of each of the five days.

* Pray the Morning Prayer.

* Read and reflect on the Thought for the Day and its meaning for your life.

* Commit the Thought for the Day to memory.

* At the end of the day, reserve fifteen minutes for journaling and prayer. In your journal, reflect on and write about times when you were able to emulate St. Francis's love for Lady Poverty as lived through love of God and neighbor.

* Conclude with the Evening Prayer.

*day*ONE

Morning Prayer

Father Most Holy,
You bring light to my day and guide me in your providence;
    walk with me today along the path of your love.
When we meet hatred, Lord, be with me;
    help me to sow your love.
    Always.

Evening Prayer

Creator God,
I long to be near you.
Bring me your light so that I may have knowledge,
    and inflame my heart with your love.
Live with me both on earth and in heaven,
    for without you there is no good.

THOUGHT FOR THE DAY
Do not promote yourself over the good the Lord works through you.

*day*TWO

Morning Prayer

Abba, Father,
Your beloved Son revealed your Holy Name.
Increase my knowledge of you so that I can grasp
    the depth of your goodness,
    the beauty of your promises,
    the brilliance of your majesty,
    and the mercy of your judgments.
As I seek to understand you and your ways,
    help me to be understood.

Evening Prayer

Glorious God,
Live in me.
Bring me to your kingdom that I might
    see you clearly,
    love you perfectly,
    be blessed in your company,
    and enjoy you forever.
Let my life in you
    lead others to your kingdom of peace.

THOUGHT FOR THE DAY
A worldly spirit loves to talk a lot and do nothing. The spirit of God, on the other hand, inspires us to humility, patience, perfect simplicity, and true peace of heart.

*day*THREE

Morning Prayer

Our Father, comfort me.
Help me to do your will.
Help me to love you
    with my whole heart by thinking of you,
    with my whole mind by seeking your glory in everything,
    with all of my strength in the service of your love alone.
Help me to love others
    by encouraging them to love you as best they can,
    by rejoicing in their good fortune,
    by sympathizing with their misfortune.
Our Father, comfort us.
Help us to do your will.

Evening Prayer

Savior Lord,
The gift of your love is my daily bread.
How odd it seems that I know your love
    when I am belittled,
    when I am alienated,
    when I am frustrated,
    or when my whole being is racked with pain.
And then I remember how you suffered for me
    on a cross of love.
Thank you, Lord, for this day.
Keep me grateful for all my gifts,
    especially for the gift of your own life.

THOUGHT FOR THE DAY
*We are brothers and sisters of the Lord when we do the
will of the Father who is in heaven.*

---

*day*FOUR

Morning Prayer

Holy Redeemer,
Your compassion envelops my failings.
Forgive me of yesterday's sins:
    my stubbornness,
    my callousness,
    my pride.
Help me to do better today:
    to grow in new ways,
    to feel the pain of others,
    to live in humble thanksgiving for your goodness.
I make this prayer through the intercession
    of the Blessed Virgin Mary and all your saints.

Evening Prayer

Lord,
Help me to forgive perfectly
    so that I may love those who trespass against me.
I know that I cannot do this for my own sake;
    help me to do it because it pleases you.
Help me to understand that the wounds they inflict on me
    flow from the pain of their own wounds.
Hear my prayer for my enemies:
    for their well-being,
    for their conversion,
    that they may find solace in you.
Hear my prayer for myself
    that I will return no evil for evil
    and that I remain ever anxious to serve you
    by serving the least of your children.

THOUGHT FOR THE DAY
It is in pardoning that we are pardoned.

---

*day*FIVE

Morning Prayer

Father Almighty,
Keep me close to you and your Son.
Help me to avoid the test of faith whether
    hidden or obvious,
        sudden or prolonged.
Save me from evil.
Guide me in my prayer through the help of the Holy Spirit.

Evening Prayer

Glory Be
Glory be to the Father,
and to the Son,
and to the Holy Spirit:
    as it was in the beginning,
    is now,
    and ever shall be,
    world without end.
Amen.

THOUGHT FOR THE DAY
Our labor here is brief, but the reward is eternal. Do not be disturbed by the clamor of the world, which passes like a shadow.

---

the *peace prayer* of St. Francis

Lord, make me an instrument of your
    peace:
where there is hatred, let me sow love;
where there is injury, pardon;
where there is doubt, faith;
where there is despair, hope;
where there is darkness, light;
and where there is sadness, joy.

O Divine Master, grant that I may not so
    much seek
to be consoled as to console,
to be understood, as to understand,
to be loved, as to love.
For it is in giving that we receive,
    it is in pardoning that we are
        pardoned,
    and it is in dying that we are born to
        eternal life.

Living
*f*ortitude

*T*he dictionary defines fortitude as "strength of mind that allows one to endure pain or adversity with courage." In fact, courage has often been synonymous with fortitude—the Church Fathers even using the two words interchangeably.

Fortitude is sustained by Christ's promise: "In the world you will have trouble, but take courage, I have conquered the world" (John 16:33).

The courage necessary to take up your cross and follow Christ is not a one-time event saved for the end of your life. Rather, this is a daily challenge to face the suffering, trials, and persecutions that come your way.

Shortly after his commitment to discipleship, St. Francis faced a test that required fortitude. He was forced to make a dramatic choice between his previous life of money, possessions, and fast living and his newfound life of poverty. Heartfelt in itself, Francis's choice was compounded in difficulty because it meant choosing discipleship over his family.

Stripping off his clothes and leaving his money in a heap in the plaza before his father, Francis accepted alienation from his family as the price of discipleship.

Francis immediately felt the physical stings of his chosen poverty. The discomfort of being wet and cold was part of his daily existence as he forged the life of a hermit.

Primarily, Francis courageously persevered in remaining true to his mission of humble service and of making living the gospel a way of life. He feared being pampered. Perhaps his true mark was living his initial calling to the end. The stigmata of Christ's wounds and his courageous journey, riddled with pain, to Sister Death were the ultimate testaments to his fortitude.

You have the same opportunity as St. Francis to commit with fortitude to the dreams and passions of your life.

First, identify your dreams and passions. What are some of the things that you love to the point of committing most of your time and energy to them? At this stage in your life, you have the chance to make your dreams come true. If you could accomplish any dream in your life, what would it be? The only rule to consider is that your dream must be humanly possible.

How might your passions and dreams involve your Christian discipleship?

If you have a passion for teaching, did you ever consider teaching underprivileged children?

If you have a passion for the fine arts, did you ever think about composing a song or painting a scene in praise of God?

If you have a passion for athletics, did you ever think of speaking out in word and example against the evils of drug abuse?

The virtue of fortitude can help you remain firm through difficulties and constant in the pursuit of the good. It can enable you to conquer fear, even the fear of death, as you endure trials along the way.

In Christ, your dreams can become reality. And with fortitude they can be accomplished.

To start, read and reflect on the following list of twenty-five projects. Many of these involve difficult challenges or reading about others who have conquered seemingly insurmountable odds. Choose at least two or three of the projects to enact. Pray along the way for the virtue of fortitude.

Twenty-five Project Ideas for Teens—Fortitude

The following project ideas suggest some radical ideas for Christian discipleship in the spirit of St. Francis of Assisi's acceptance of Jesus' call to take up his cross and follow. Many of the ideas may only whet your appetite for what can be possible in your life in the future. Others you can enact now.

Use the project ideas in the following way:

Read through the entire list.

Write up a plan for how your dreams and passions in life might translate to a radical form of Christian discipleship.

Enact—either on your own or with a group of peers—one of the projects that is doable for your state in life right now.

1. Work with a parish youth minister to create a space for teens to hang out after school and on weekends. This space may be at a parish church (not necessarily your own parish) or may be in a room at a park or recreational building, school, or library. Arrange for donations of books, games, a refrigerator, and the like. Help to organize staffing and supervision of the space. Work to develop programming that helps to involve teens in helping others.

2. Sign a public pledge to be abstinent from sex until marriage. Promote abstinence as a healthy and moral life choice. Arrange to hear a speaker on the topics of chastity and abstinence before marriage.

3. Explore ways to work for solidarity and justice among all people in the world by examining the links at the Catholic Relief Services website: www.catholicrelief.org/get_involved/high_school/index.cfm. Take the lead in initiating one of the efforts described at your school or parish.

4. Create a theater group that uses songs, skits, personal testimony, and the like to witness faith in Jesus Christ. Travel with the group, performing before youth groups, school assemblies, and at church and civic fairs and bazaars.

5. Youth Service America is an alliance of over three hundred agencies designed to provide volunteer opportunities for people from ages five to twenty-five. Visit the Youth Service America website at www.ysa.org. Within the site, type your zip code to find out about service opportunities in your area.

6. Offer support to those infected with HIV or suffering from AIDS. Many fundraising and awareness efforts are sponsored by Catholic Charities. Contact the local agency in your area. See www.catholiccharitiesinfo.org/jobs/volunteer.cfm.

7. Read about basketball coach Jim Valvano, who fought a brave battle with cancer and established The V Foundation prior to his death. The motto of the foundation, "Don't give up, don't ever give up," is representative of the virtue of Christian fortitude. See www.jimmyv.org. Note especially Coach Valvano's acceptance speech at the 1993 ESPY awards.

8. Become a "lunch buddy" with a younger student or peer who might benefit from your company. For example, consider a student with special physical needs who may appreciate a change in company or venue. A younger student may benefit from your mentoring involving academic and social issues.

9. Begin a challenging physical fitness program that incorporates healthy eating and prayer. Set a goal (e.g., running a 10 K race, increasing weightlifting reps, hiking to the top of a high peak) and work to achieve it. Pray to the Holy Spirit for the increase in the gift of fortitude.

10. Start or participate in an ongoing morning prayer group with some of your peers. Meet near the school flagpole prior to the first period of the day. Arrange for a new leader each day. Pray for peace, faith, and justice both in your community and throughout the world. Share a reading from the Bible.

11. Research the charisms of a Franciscan community for either men or women. Reflect on how you can incorporate these charisms into your life right now. Also, note the requirements for a lifelong Franciscan vocation (including vocations as a lay third order Franciscan) beginning with the discernment process. See, for example, www.franciscanfriarstor.com/resources/Franciscan_ Federation (with links to particular Franciscan communities for men and women).

12. Sponsor a Christmas dinner for the homeless and needy in your community. Schedule the dinner on an evening between Thanksgiving and Christmas so as not to duplicate other similar efforts. Secure a place with enough seating (and preferably a kitchen) like a parish or school auditorium. Arrange for food donations from the local community. The main course should be a cooked turkey that should be delivered to the meal site just prior to the start of the event. Also secure donations for the other parts of the meal (e.g. vegetables, mashed potatoes, cranberry, desserts, coffee, milk, etc.). Work with other peers to serve the meal. Arrange also for meals to be delivered to the homebound.

13. Read about the Poor Clare nuns at www.poorclare.org. On the website, look for the Poor Clare community nearest to you. Arrange a visit to share in communal prayer or work with the nuns. If no community is nearby, write to a sister asking her to share ideas for personal prayer and service in your area.

14. Clean out your closet and dresser of unneeded clothing. Encourage other family members to do the same. Donate this clothing to a St. Vincent de Paul or Salvation Army agency in your area.

15. Franciscans International, a non-governmental agency of the United Nations, lists opportunities for youth to volunteer with local and worldwide justice issues. See www.franciscansinternational.org for more information.

16. Pray the Peace Prayer of St. Francis (see page 50). Initiate your own plan for the week to be an instrument of the Lord's peace.

17. As St. Francis once worked to repair St. Damian's Church at Assisi, gather a group of peers to do a Saturday afternoon of chores at a local parish most in need.

18. Organize a peace symposium for elementary age students. Develop a presentation or produce a skit depicting several ways to resolve typical grade school conflicts peacefully. Plan to share a prayer for peace to conclude the event.

19. Arrange to view the video *St. Francis of Assisi* (Teleketics, 1988). It presents a powerful story of his life from the time of his conversion to his death. Contact your diocesan media center for information on rental.

20. Complete a free registration for the Life Teen chat room (see www.lifeteen.org/teentalk.asp). Spend some time discussing with other teens issues in yours and their lives that demand courage and fortitude. Keep a journal or log of things you learn from the discussion as well as any questions you might need to have answered outside of the chat room.

21. Rent and watch the DVD or video of *Dead Man Walking*, the story of Sr. Helen Prejean and her ministry to a convicted murderer on death row. Discuss with peers the courage various characters display throughout the movie.

22. Correspond with a person whose occupation puts them in danger (e.g., police officer, firefighter, soldier) as they protect others. Ask the person to explain the motivation for what they do and to define what fortitude means to them.

23. Volunteer at a pet refuge or animal shelter. Pray for the well-being of the animals as St. Francis would have.

24. Meet with a partner. Each of you print your five most prized possessions on separate strips of paper. Place the strips face down in front of you. Take turns drawing your partner's strip. Pause to discuss what your life would be like if you really lost that possession. Continue the discussion to involve losing dreams, health, people in your life. Compare this exercise with Jesus' call to "lose his life for my sake and that of the gospel" (see Mark 8:34-38).

25. "When the going gets tough, the tough get going" is one saying that points to the importance of fortitude. Nowhere is this more apparent than in athletic competition, where mental toughness often plays as great a role in success as physical talents. For any athletic activity you engage in, concentrate for the next two weeks on being courageous and determined, following your coach's admonitions to give one hundred percent of your effort.